Plutón y los Planetas
Pluto and the Planets

by
Diana DeBerry

for my little world, All the kids that made this whole thing possible. thank you all for your inspiration and help.

use the QR code to see us in Real Life

Se los nombres de las Planetas!
I know the names of our planets!

It's me, Pluto.
Soy Plutón.

Today, I'm going to show you
Hoy, te voy a enseñarlos

Hello, Pluto!
Hola Plutón.
Are you a planet?
Eres Planeta?

I'm ready to visit the solar system. shall we?

Estoy preparado a visitar nuestro systema solar. Listo?

Let Start with the Sun
Empesamos con el Sol

https://webyblox.com/viewAR.php?id=128>

Our star that gives light to everyone
Nuestro estrella que da luz a todos

Meet Mercury
Es Mercurio
the smallest planet.
El planeta mas pequeno.

The closest to the sun
Lo mas cerca al sol

Mercury
Mercurio

https://webyblox.com/viewAR.php?id=108

takes 88 Earth days to have a year.

Toma 88 dias terrenas para un año ayi

But its entire day takes Earth 176 days to clear.

Perro un dia ayi toma 176 dias aqui

I have a question to raise.
Tengo una pregunta

Shouldn't years take longer than days?

No debe años tomar mas tiempo que dias?

Well, that's not always the case.

No siempre es asi

Planets move in two ways.

Planetas mueven en dos formas.

Primero en su propio Axis
First on its own axis

Like a spinning dancer
como un bailador dando vuelta

Segundo se mueven alrededor del sol.
Second they move around the sun on a path called the orbit.
Se llama su órbita.

Doy vuelta lentamente en mi axis asi
mis dias son mas largas.

I turn slowly on my axis so
my days are longer.

In orbit I'm quick, so a year
takes shorter!

Pero mi órbita es rapido asi mi
ano es más corto!

https://webyblox.com/viewAR.php?id=117

Venus

Of all the planets, it rises above.

De todo los planetas se eleva por encima.

While all other planets spin its axis counterclockwise,

Mientra otras planetas gira a su axis en sentido anti-horario,

Venus turns the other way

Venus gira hacia el otro lado

different than the rest

diferente al resto

This makes the planet
Esto hace que el planeta esta

upside-down.
al revés

https://webyblox.com/viewAR.php?id=122

Planet number three
is our very own.

Planeta numero tres
es el nuestro

It is Earth,
Es la Tierra,

70% of its surface is water.

70% del superficie es Agua.

https://webyblox.com/viewAR.php?id=124

Mars, the fourth planet,

Marte, planeta número cuatro,

It's nickname is "Red".

También tiene titulo de "el planeta rojo"

Where are we off to next, Pluto?

Adonde vamos ahora, Plutón?

To the bigger planets, we go!

A planetas mas grandes, Vamos!

They're ancient debris when the planets are forming.

Son escombros antiguos cuando estaban formando los planetas.

We're in the asteroid belt you see!

Estamos en el cinturón de asteróides

Meet Jupiter!

https://webyblox.com/viewAR.php?id=125

Presentando a Júpiter!

A day is just ten hours here
but my year is 11.8 in Earth years!

Un dia es solo diez horas aquí pero
mi año es 11.8 años por la Tierra

Hydrogen and helium make
up its atmosphere.

hidrógeno y helio es su
atmósfera

https://webyblox.com/viewAR.php?id=127'

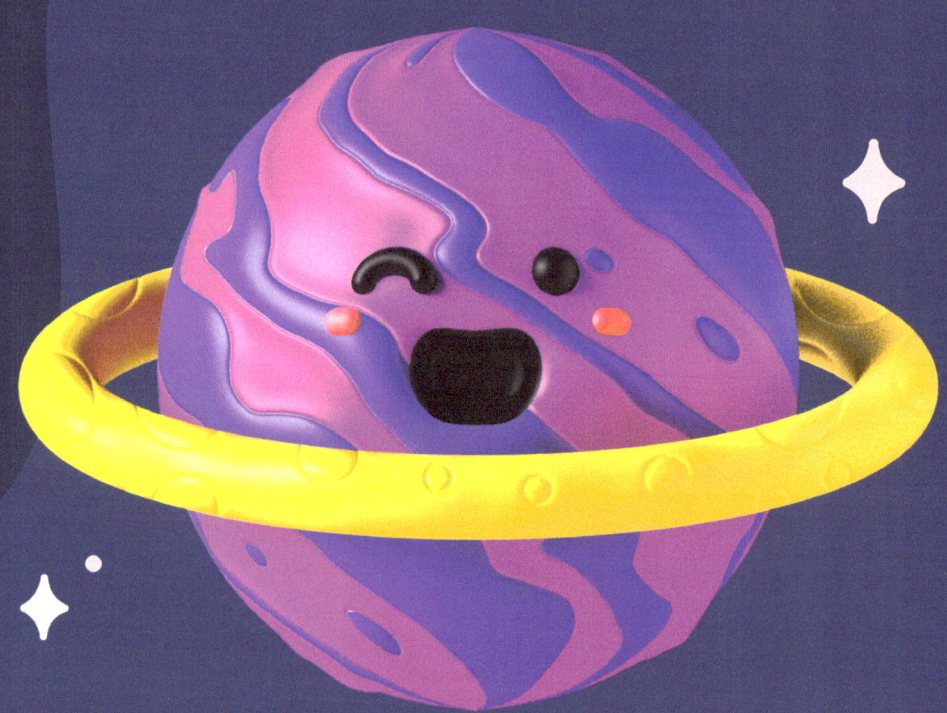

This is my pal Saturn,
Esto es mi amigo Saturno,

I have 7 wider rings all bright and icy,
first seen by Galileo Galilei!

Tengo 7 anillos brillante y helado,
Galileo Galilei lo vió primero!

Prettiest of all planets — that's me!

Planeta mas bonito - soy yo!

82 moons keep me company.

82 lunas me hacen compañía.

Nice to meet you both!
Mucho Gusto!

Hey, is it getting colder?
No les hace frio aqui?

Ah, yes because we're now near the coldest planet out here!

Es porque estamos cerca a los planetas más frias aqui!

https://webyblox.com/viewAR.php?id=131

My name is Uranus
Mi nombre es Urano

and I'm blue-green, caused by sunlight and methane.

y soy azul verde por el sol y metano

Like my neighbors I have rings, a total of 13!

Y como mis vecinos tengo anillos también, un total de 13!

Uranus, are you okay?
Estas Bien Urano?

Why are you moving sideways?

Porque estas de lado?

I move almost 90 degrees on my side. This is how I rotate and I'm alright.

Muevo a casi 90 degrados a mi lado. Es como giro y estoy bien.

We've come so far!
Estamos tan afuera!

Are we approaching another star?
estamos cerca a otro estrella?

I'm afraid not,
my friend.
But hey, here's our

no mis amigos, per aqui
esta nuestro

final planet.
planeta final

https://webyblox.com/viewAR.php?id=130

Here is Neptune,
Aqui esta Neptuno,

and it has 14 moons!
y tiene 14 lunas!

I'm a bit rocky and mostly blue and icy.
My six rings are very hard to see.

soy un poco rocoso y mayormente azul helado.
Mis anillos son difícil de ver.

That's because I'm the farthest planet.

Es porque soy el Planeta mas fuera

I'm away from the Sun by 30 astronomical units.

estoy afuera del sol 30 unidades astronómicas

https://webyblox.com/viewAR.php?id=132

Say, Pluto, you're even farther away — 39 astronomical units

Y tu Pluton, eres hasta mas fuera! 39 unidades astronómicas

Cold	Frio
Hot	Caliente
Name	Nombre
Turn/Rotate	Giro
Adonde	Where
Hello	Hola
Close	Cerca
System	Systema
Units	Unidades
Star	Estrella
See	Ver
Light	Luz
Planets	Planetas
Asteroid	Asteróid
Icy	Helado
Away	Afuera

www.ingramcontent.com/pod-product-compliance
Lightning Source LLC
LaVergne TN
LVHW072056070426
835508LV00002B/129